CAUSES OF THE CIVIL WAR

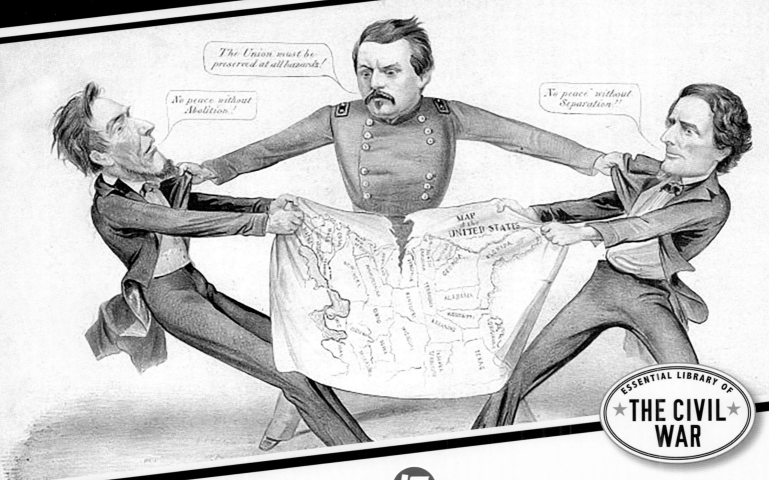

Essential Library

An Imprint of Abdo Publishing
abdopublishing.com

BY MICHAEL CAPEK

CONTENT CONSULTANT

MICHAEL DAVID COHEN
RESEARCH ASSOCIATE PROFESSOR OF HISTORY
UNIVERSITY OF TENNESSEE, KNOXVILLE

abdopublishing.com

Published by Abdo Publishing, a division of ABDO, PO Box 398166, Minneapolis, Minnesota 55439. Copyright © 2017 by Abdo Consulting Group, Inc. International copyrights reserved in all countries. No part of this book may be reproduced in any form without written permission from the publisher. Essential Library™ is a trademark and logo of Abdo Publishing.

Printed in the United States of America, North Mankato, Minnesota

052016
092016

THIS BOOK CONTAINS
RECYCLED MATERIALS

Cover Photo: Currier & Ives/Library of Congress
Interior Photos: Currier & Ives/Library of Congress, 1, 4, 89, 99 (bottom right); North Wind Picture Archives, 7, 12, 15, 22, 25, 27, 39, 47, 53, 55, 60, 62, 75, 80, 83, 87, 90, 98, 99 (top); Library of Congress, 8, 17, 30, 35, 41, 42, 51, 53, 56, 67, 69, 83, 99 (bottom left); Willard/iStockphoto/Thinkstock, 21; Timothy H. O'Sullivan/Library of Congress, 32; G. W. Bromley & Co./Library of Congress, 45; AS400 DB/Corbis, 52; American School (19th century)/Private Collection/Peter Newark American Pictures/ Bridgeman Art, 65; Alexander Gardner/Library of Congress, 70, 95; W. H. Rease/Library of Congress, 76; Mathew B. Brady/ Library of Congress, 79; Paul Philippoteaux/Library of Congress, 96

Editor: Susan E. Hamen
Series Designers: Kelsey Oseid and Maggie Villaume

Cataloging-in-Publication Data

Names: Capek, Michael, author.
Title: Civil War causes / by Michael Capek.
Description: Minneapolis, MN : Abdo Publishing, [2017] | Series: Essential library
    of the Civil War | Includes bibliographical references and index.
Identifiers: LCCN 2015960306 | ISBN 9781680782752 (lib. bdg.) |
    ISBN 9781680774641 (ebook)
Subjects: LCSH: United States--History--Civil War, 1861-1865--Causes--
    Juvenile literature.
Classification: DDC 973.7/11--dc23
LC record available at http://lccn.loc.gov/2015860306

CONTENTS

Construction of the interior was still underway when Fort Sumter became the scene of the start of the Civil War on April 12, 1861.

SHOWDOWN AT FORT SUMTER: THE BRINK OF WAR

The sea in Charleston Harbor was calm that cold winter evening, December 26, 1860. At Fort Moultrie overlooking the harbor, though, the situation was anything but calm. While most people in Charleston, South Carolina, were resting from their Christmas celebrations, the soldiers inside Moultrie's walls were busy making preparations of a different kind.

Under the watchful eyes of their commander, US Army major Robert Anderson, the entire garrison, made up of two companies of approximately 40 men each, gathered whatever guns and supplies they could carry. In the semidarkness, the soldiers worked feverishly, getting ready for a daring water retreat across Charleston Harbor.

To Anderson, deserting his fort seemed wise under the circumstances. Only six days earlier, South Carolina had declared its independence from the United States of America, officially seceding from the Union. To secessionists, this meant that, though war had not been formally declared, federal troops in South Carolina were essentially in foreign territory. Other Southern states were also preparing to secede, and in fact, armed groups that supported the formation of the Confederate States of America had already seized all federal forts in the area except four. Two of those were in Charleston—Moultrie and Fort Sumter.

There was strong reason to believe local rebels would soon attempt to take the last two forts. Anderson and his men had heard and seen troubling things over the past few weeks. He felt certain that as soon as holiday celebrations were over, an attack would come. Anderson later said he felt like "a sheep tied, watching the butcher sharpening a knife to cut his throat."[1]

Sumter was a pentagon-shaped island fortress at the entrance to Charleston Harbor. Though construction of the fort was unfinished, its 50-foot- (15 m) high and 5-foot- (1.5 m) thick brick and mortar walls and other fortifications were complete. It had strong casements armed with three levels of powerful guns. Anderson figured the odds of his and his companies' survival in the new year were far better at rock-solid Sumter than at Moultrie.

Anderson's plan was to move the garrison in two waves. A small group of volunteers would remain in Moultrie, manning its 32-pound (15 kg) guns, to cover each wave in case of an attack. Attack was possible, even likely, since armed patrol boats constantly watched the harbor. The rearguard would disable Moultrie's guns so they couldn't be used against them as they made their own dash for the safety of Sumter.

Carrying the garrison's carefully folded flag under his arm, Anderson led the first company from the fort as soon as darkness fell. His men quickly loaded the three boats waiting in a cove below the fort and began rowing across the harbor.

Prior to the Civil War, Major Robert Anderson served in the US Army during the Black Hawk War of 1832 and the Second Seminole War (1835–1842).

Halfway across, a Charleston guard boat loomed suddenly in the darkness, heading straight for them. Two of Anderson's boats slipped away before they were seen, but a third was cut off and forced to stop dead in the water while the patrol boat bore down on it. The men in the small boat waited as the steam-powered boat drew closer, then slowed to a halt. Back in Fort Moultrie, the rearguard manning the artillery thought of firing for a few breathless moments. Fortunately, though, the harbor patrol boat soon moved off and disappeared back into the darkness.

Upon arriving at Fort Sumter, Major Anderson reverently hoisted the flag he had brought from Fort Moultrie.

The federal soldiers rowed frantically on to Sumter as the relieved artillerymen of the rearguard watched.

By first light the next morning, Anderson's entire command had successfully made the crossing, unloaded supplies, and established defensive positions inside Sumter. At sunrise, Anderson ordered the flag raised on the high mast. The men cheered as the Stars and Stripes rose and the band played "The Star-Spangled Banner."

Visible for miles, the fluttering flag was the first thing many Charleston residents saw when they arose that morning. Word quickly spread of Anderson's bold maneuver. Fortifying Sumter and making a stand there was a blatant act of war, many people cried. To the delight of most of the town's residents, rebel military leaders in Charleston turned out all available militia and trained all guns on Fort Sumter. General P. G. T. Beauregard, Confederate commander

GENERAL P. G. T. BEAUREGARD

P. G. T. Beauregard, the general in charge of Confederate forces in Charleston, was the son of a proud, aristocratic French family and a devoted fan of French general Napoleon Bonaparte. Like his idol, Beauregard dreamed of leading armies to glory in battle, and he achieved that goal, in part. His role in the Sumter siege and the First Battle of Bull Run made him the Confederacy's first great military hero. But the general's enormous ego and pompous style did not sit well with Confederate president Jefferson Davis. In 1862, Davis relieved Beauregard of his command and assigned him to minor posts for the rest of the war.

of forces in Charleston, sent a message to Anderson. Unless he surrendered immediately, the fort would be attacked. And to show he meant business, Beauregard ordered batteries around the harbor to fire at a federal ship when it appeared to bring much needed supplies, driving it away. Despite the display of aggression, Anderson did not fire back, nor did he surrender. His orders were to hold his position and not fight unless the fort itself was fired upon. That would, of course, mean war. Neither side, now that the moment had arrived, seemed willing to begin one. With cannons loaded and ready, both sides waited for orders from their superiors while the fate of the nation hung in the balance.

The showdown at Fort Sumter was the last in a long series of events that led to the American Civil War (1861–1865). That conflict, the bloodiest and most destructive ever fought on US soil, cost an estimated 625,000 lives.[2] That is nearly as many as the combined number of American soldiers who died in all the other wars in which the United States has ever been

FRIENDS BECOME ENEMIES

Confederate general P. G. T. Beauregard, commander of Confederate forces in Charleston, and Union major Robert Anderson were actually friends. While Anderson was an artillery instructor at West Point in the 1830s, Beauregard had been one of his best and brightest students, and each still held the other in high esteem. They exchanged friendly notes and even bottles of wine via messengers before their Sumter encounter finally turned deadly serious. The situation represented in a small way the tragedy of the entire Civil War—former countrymen, friends, and even family members could not find a way to avoid attacking and killing one another.

involved. Some recent evidence suggests the Civil War death toll could be as high as 750,000.[3]

What caused such unbridled rage and hostility to erupt in 1861 between people who shared a common history, language, government, and culture? Why did citizens of the formerly united states begin shooting and killing one another, even though leaders of both sides claimed to hate war?

The answers to these questions have been the subject of study and debate for more than 150 years. Nearly all historians today agree the main cause of the war may be summed up in one word: *slavery*. Certainly, few people who went to war in 1861, or the leaders who took them there, disagreed fundamentally with that assessment. Still, explaining how disagreement over that one practice could cause such a catastrophic event is not a simple matter. The road to Fort Sumter and the brink of war was not a straight path. It was a long, winding road, a series of interconnected events and various shifts in attitudes that eventually sparked the costliest war in US history.

In a search for the causes of any war, the best place to start is at the beginning, looking for the seeds of strife. To find them one has to go back to the early years of European settlement in North America.

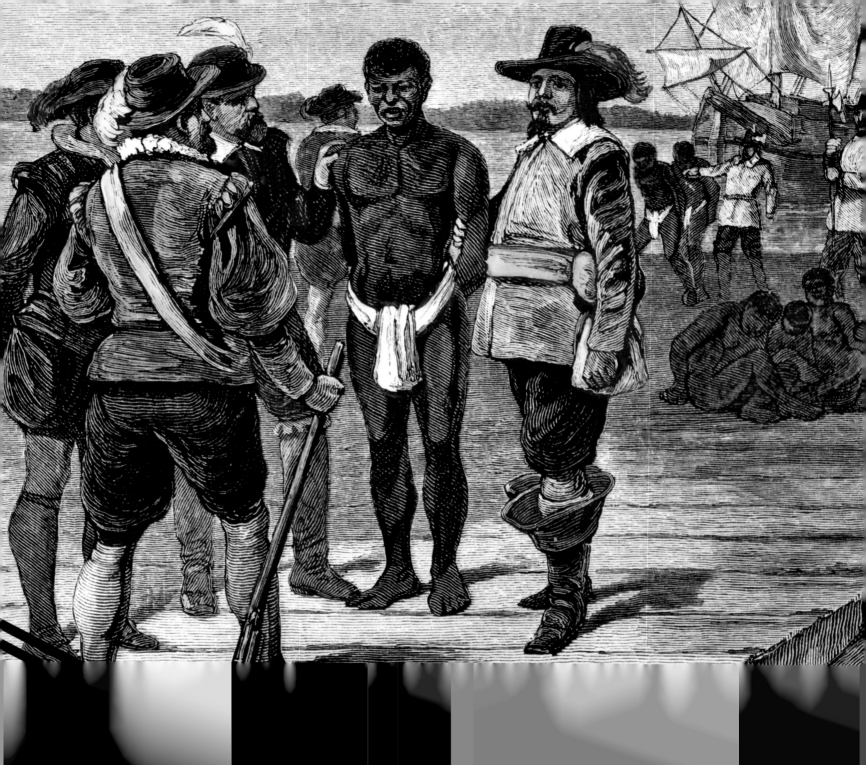

SLAVERY IN A "MORE PERFECT UNION"

Slavery came to the colonies as early as 1619 when Dutch traders delivered African slaves to Jamestown, Virginia. The captives were said to be indentured servants, which meant they would work until they had paid off their transportation and support fees, earning their freedom. But in 1670, the Virginia House of Burgesses adopted a policy that declared non-Christian servants "imported into the colony by shipping shall be slaves for their lives."[1]

After that, the number of slaves arriving in America increased rapidly. In 1700, more than 25,000 African slaves were in bondage throughout the 13 original colonies.[2] As the century progressed, many New England shippers grew wealthy supplying slaves to the colonies, particularly in the region known as the Deep South. In the Deep South, which included Georgia, Alabama, South Carolina, Mississippi, and Louisiana, the warmer climate made large-scale farming a nearly year-round enterprise. The plantation culture, with slavery as its lifeblood, became a fixture in the American South. Assumptions of white superiority, economic interest, and the idea that slavery would civilize and Christianize supposedly savage Africans helped perpetuate the institution from generation to generation.

The lives of slaves in America varied widely depending on where they were. Living quarters, food, and treatment in some locations were better than in others. The majority of slaves in the South worked in the fields, where they faced perhaps the harshest conditions. They often worked in the hot sun from sunrise to sunset and sometimes longer, if there was a full moon. Any show of resistance was not tolerated, and runaways, if caught, faced beatings, humiliation, or confinement. House servants and those with certain skills—blacksmiths, carpenters, tailors, shoemakers, cooks, or musicians, for instance—often lived better lives. Some even became overseers of other slaves. Still, nothing could make up for the absence of freedom or basic rights and the ever-present realization that one had no hope for a better future. Slaves were dehumanized and not allowed to marry or become educated. Many were savagely beaten or even raped.

Due to harsh working conditions, poor treatment, and high death rates of infants

THE FOUNDING FATHERS

In 1776, as the American Revolutionary War (1775–1783) raged, Thomas Jefferson wrote, "We hold these truths to be self-evident, that all men are created equal and endowed by their Creator with certain unalienable rights."[3] At the time, there were more than four million slaves in America.[4] Jefferson himself owned approximately 200 of them.[5] George Washington owned more than 300.[6]

When representatives of the Continental Congress met in Philadelphia, Pennsylvania, on June 11, 1776, to draft the Declaration of Independence, slavery was a controversial issue. In order to convince Southern colonies, where slavery was most prevalent, to accept the terms of the agreement and join a confederation of states in the war of independence against Great Britain, delegates compromised. In the end, references to slavery were cut from the document, including those condemning Great Britain's history of slave trading.

THE DECLARATION OF DISUNION?

After expressing Americans' right to "Life, Liberty, and the Pursuit of Happiness," the Declaration of Independence states,

Whenever any Form of Government becomes destructive of these ends, it is the Right of the People to alter or to abolish it, and to institute new Government, laying its foundation on such principles and organizing its powers in such form, as to them shall seem most likely to effect their Safety and Happiness.[7]

Southern secessionists would later cite this paragraph to prove their right to secede from the Union and form a confederacy of their own.

The Founding Fathers omitted language regarding slavery from the Declaration of Independence to encourage Southern representatives to sign it.

But these representatives could not sidestep the slavery issue for long. During the summer of 1787, the State House in Philadelphia was the site of another gathering of 55 distinguished delegates from most of the states in the newly independent United States.[8] The representatives, known collectively today as the Founding Fathers, were there to perform a critical task—create a new centralized, federal government and a constitution to guide it.

The states had banded together during the Revolutionary War for their mutual support and protection under the Articles of Confederation and Perpetual Union. Despite its grand title, some thought this agreement was woefully ineffective. They thought it was critical to the nation's survival that 13 separate states become "we the people of the United States," and form what the introductory words of the new national Constitution would call "a more perfect Union."[9]

The Constitution was signed on September 17, 1787. For several turbulent months, the representatives argued and bargained. In the end, all the states ratified the Constitution. But after the dust settled, one important issue

THE NORTHWEST ORDINANCE

The treaty ending the war between Great Britain and the United States, signed in 1783, awarded the new nation a vast tract of land north of the Ohio River and east of the Mississippi. Delegates to the Constitutional Convention adopted a set of rules known as the Northwest Ordinance to govern this region and any future states formed from it. One of these rules said, "there shall be neither slavery nor involuntary servitude" in these territories or states.[10] Another article added later required escaped slaves found there to be returned to their owners. Adoption of these seemingly conflicting laws helped slave and antislave states avoid conflict during the nation's founding, but it sowed the seeds of future, bitter confrontations.

remained unresolved, one that would continue to trouble and eventually divide the nation in the coming century.

A CONSTITUTIONAL COMPROMISE

The disagreement developed during discussions about how many representatives each state would be permitted in Congress. Southern states made it clear they wanted to count slaves as part of their population figures. Doing so would give the states more representatives, which meant more voting power and greater control of the future government. Northern states, which had few if any slaves, objected, often voicing their displeasure with depictions of slaveholders as dealers in human misery and cruelty.

In the face of these attacks, Southern delegates finally drew a line in the sand. Speaking mainly for his own state of South Carolina, but also for the entire region, John Rutledge declared the real question was not whether slavery was right or wrong. The true question before the convention was "whether the

AVOIDING THE ISSUE?

Framers of the 1787 Constitution avoided referring to slavery directly. Instead of saying escaping slaves must be returned to their owners, Article IV reads:

No Person held to Service or Labour in one State, under the Laws thereof, escaping into another, shall, in Consequence of any Law or Regulation therein, be discharged from such Service or Labour, but shall be delivered up on Claim of the Party to whom such Service or Labour may be due.[11]

This Fugitive Slave Law would become perhaps the most controversial (and disobeyed) law of the 1800s.

Southern states shall or shall not be parties to the Union."[12] Simply put, the South would not join a nation whose Constitution banned slavery.

With the very existence of a united country hanging in the balance, Northern and Southern delegates did what they did in 1776. They compromised. It was agreed that Southern states could count each slave as three-fifths of a person in their population totals. In return, Southern states had to agree to stop importing slaves in 1808. After that, Congress would have the authority to ban or continue slavery as it saw fit. As a bonus for the South, as part of another agreement made in the soon-to-be-dissolved Confederation Congress, the new Constitution would also contain a law requiring that escaped slaves be returned to their owners.

As Alexander Hamilton pointed out later, without this compromise, "no Union could possibly have been formed."[13] Still, some delegates felt profound sadness and anger as they signed a document that maintained the captivity and enslavement of human beings. Many Americans felt it was a cruel irony that a nation founded on principles of freedom and justice continued to allow and even support slavery.

THE THREE-FIFTHS RULE

The three-fifths rule did indeed give the South more control over the government. From 1789 to 1861, all presidents were Southern slaveholders except John Adams and John Quincy Adams. The South's three-fifths advantage gave it more electoral votes than it would have had without the rule. Also during that time, two-thirds of the Speakers of the House were Southerners. As a result, with the help of a small but powerful block of Northerners, supporters of slavery usually controlled the federal government.

The Constitution laid the framework for the laws of the United States. Yet African Americans received no rights or protection under it.

As the new nation moved confidently into a new century, two crucial questions remained unanswered: What happens when state and federal governments disagree? What options remain if compromise fails?

EXPANDING NATION, EXPANDING PROBLEMS

In 1803, Napoleon Bonaparte was desperate for money to continue his quest for domination in Europe. Early that year, he surprised a US ambassador by asking how much the United States would pay for France's massive Louisiana Territory. In July, Congress approved the purchase of Louisiana—a territory encompassing 828,000 square miles (2,250,000 square km), approximately one-third of North America—for a mere $15 million.[1] Almost overnight, the United States expanded to twice its original size. President Jefferson declared grandly that the United States was about to become "the Empire of Liberty," and he sent explorers

Meriwether Lewis and William Clark to explore the vast western regions, which stretched almost to the Pacific Ocean.[2]

Few white Americans doubted the president's prediction. A pervading sense of excitement seized the nation. This overwhelming feeling of righteous entitlement to possess and settle the land to the west soon became the "Manifest Destiny," a sense that a divine power had decreed the nation's right to claim the entire continent.[3]

Not everyone was optimistic about all this new land. After the end of John Adams's administration and the Louisiana Purchase deal under President Jefferson, many New Englanders felt isolated and worried. Southerners, led by Jefferson, were taking over and making all the decisions. Sooner or later, some New Englanders feared, Southern slave owners would decide to take the institution of slavery into the new lands. It was time to stop spreading out and give some thought to who would control those territories.

Many New England states still had thriving business relations with the United Kingdom. They were alarmed when President James Madison confronted the United Kingdom, whose naval power was interfering with American trade. Then, Madison decided to send federal troops to invade the rich lands of Canada, seemingly there for the taking. New England protested and refused to help pay for the ensuing War of 1812 (1812–1815). Threats by some in New England to leave the Union ended when future president Andrew Jackson won a resounding

General Andrew Jackson paraded through the streets of New Orleans, celebrating victory over British troops in New Orleans, Louisiana, and the United Kingdom and the United States signed a treaty ending the war. While the nation celebrated, though, many New Englanders did not join in.

A period of relative goodwill among the states followed, often called "the Era of Good Feelings" (1817–1825).[4] The nation continued to grow as Indiana, Mississippi, Illinois, and Alabama entered the Union. The additions brought the total number of slave states and Free States to a balance of 11 each.[5]

THE MISSOURI COMPROMISE

Feelings of fellowship and unity did not last long. When Missouri applied for admission to the Union as a slave state in 1819, it set off yet another argument between Free States in the North and slave states in the South. The problem this time was that most of the Missouri territory lay north of the Ohio River. The Northwest Ordinance of 1787, signed on July 13, 1787, outlawed slavery in the territory north of the Ohio River, but it did not restrict future states formed in that territory from becoming slave states. Missouri becoming a slave state would upset the delicate balance between slave states and Free States. The two sides squared off in Congress, the official, constitutionally empowered overseer of new territories. There, free- and slave-state senators engaged in a round of bitter name-calling and debates over the morality of slavery that did nothing to solve the problem at hand. After all, the debate was not just about Missouri.

MAP OF THE
UNITED STATES
1820
SHOWING THE
MISSOURI COMPROMISE

NAT TURNER'S REBELLION

Believing God had given him signs, in August 1831, Nat Turner, a Virginia slave, organized one of the bloodiest slave revolts in US history. During a weeklong rampage, Turner, leading a band of 50–75 other slaves, murdered at least 55 white people, including his own master and his master's family. Turner and his followers were captured and hanged. In the hysterical aftermath, more than 200 black people were rounded up and executed. Most had taken no part in the Nat Turner rebellion.[6]

Soon other states would be carved from the vast western territory. Congressmen wondered if they would have to fight the same battle over slavery before each state was admitted.

Senator Henry Clay of Kentucky stepped in with an idea to stop the verbal feuding. The Missouri Compromise, as it was called, essentially voided the old Northwest Ordinance. In its place, a new plan drew a new boundary line north of the Ohio River that continued westward along the parallel of latitude 36°30' north. Any future state south of this line would be open to slavery. Any state north of it would be free, with the exception of Missouri. With its southern border on the line, Missouri would be admitted as a slave state. Maine would be admitted as a nonslave state. President James Monroe signed the Missouri Compromise on March 6, 1820. When the deal was done, many heaved a sigh of relief because the fragile balance of power between free and slave states had been restored. However, others despaired that slavery was again allowed to flourish in the land of the free.

THE AMERICAN COLONIZATION SOCIETY

Members of the American Colonization Society (ACS), organized in 1816, believed one solution to the slavery problem was to free the slaves and return them to Africa. They raised money and bought land in Africa, where they founded the colony of Liberia. A few free blacks moved there with ACS assistance, but many more refused to go. They did not want to leave family and familiar surroundings behind, and some suspected that racism was behind ACS's efforts. Some members of the ACS did see colonization as a way to rid the United States of freed African Americans. However, many more honestly believed returning former slaves and freedmen to Africa would allow them to prosper. Most of these slaves had been born in the United States and had never even been to Africa. Despite the refusal of many to "return" to Africa, the organization continued its work well into the 1900s.

"A FIRE BELL IN THE NIGHT"

Former president Jefferson, now in retirement at Monticello, his Virginia plantation, watched the Missouri debate with mounting dread. As a Virginian, he blamed New Englanders for holding what he considered extreme, rigid attitudes about the South and its increasingly valuable institution. At the same time, though, he readily admitted that both sides had contributed to the bitterness he saw enveloping the government. He felt strongly that the fight over slavery in Missouri was only the beginning. Western expansion was sure to set off more confrontations over slavery. He had even begun to have serious doubts "that our union would be of long duration" unless the slavery question was resolved.[7]

Jefferson understood the vital role slavery played in the Southern economy. Emancipation of the slaves, which some New Englanders demanded, would be catastrophic for the South and the entire nation. More and more, all the clamor and name-calling in Washington, DC, over the slavery issue sounded to him "like a fire bell in the night, signaling the death knell of the Union."[8] Jefferson believed gradual changes were the answer. He advocated for better living conditions for slaves and less physical punishment. He also supported the implementation of freedom for those born into slavery after a certain number of years. Eventually, he thought abolition would be possible after these gradual steps.

To avoid a collapse of the South's economy, Jefferson supported a gradual plan for the abolition of slavery.

TARIFFS AND NULLIFICATION

In 1828 and 1832, new tariffs were enacted to protect Northern industries that were losing business due to cheaper imported goods. Although these new tariffs helped the Northern economy, they ended up hurting business in the South. The high export taxes made it difficult for the British to buy cotton from the South. This infuriated Southern leaders. Vice President John C. Calhoun resigned his office in protest. His home state of South Carolina declared the tariffs null and void. This defiance of federal law led President Jackson to threaten to invade the state. Tensions eased when Congress lowered the tariff amount. The question of whether state governments had a right to ignore federal laws they did not like, however, remained unresolved.

The Mexican–American War (1846–1848) resulted in the acquisition of an incredibly rich and vast stretch of territory that increased the size of the United States, from 1,753,588 square miles (4,550,000 sq km) to approximately 2,400,000 square miles (6,216,000 sq km).[9] The Mexican Cession included the areas of California, New Mexico, Utah, and Texas. The settling of an Oregon boundary dispute with the United Kingdom added even more land, stretching the United States from coast to coast. However, many in New England and the growing Northwest did not support the Mexican–American War, arguing that it was a shameless grab by the US government for even more western land. Americans were finding that the expansion of the nation in pursuit of "Manifest Destiny" was bringing growing pains.

CHAPTER 4

THE CALIFORNIA QUESTION AND ANOTHER COMPROMISE

In August 1846, Pennsylvania congressman David Wilmot introduced a bill proposing to ban slavery from new western territories and all future states established from them. Predictably, antislavery advocates enthusiastically supported the proposal, and slave states furiously opposed it. After much hostile discussion, the so-called Wilmot Proviso failed to pass in the Senate. Yet a growing, vocal group of Northern legislators became determined to get Congress to ban slavery from all western states. They continued proposing antislavery resolutions at every opportunity throughout the 1840s.

Later, many people recognized the Wilmot Proviso as a dividing line between an era of relative civility and reason in Congress over the slavery issue and a period of rancor and conflict that seemed to grow in intensity with each passing year. According to historian David Goldfield, after the Wilmot Proviso, "reality scarcely made a demonstration in the Capitol. Henceforth . . . every issue seemed to touch on slavery."[1]

WILMOT AND "THE WHITE MAN'S PROVISO"

In truth, the Wilmot Proviso was motivated less by concern over slavery and more by racial bigotry. The belief that whites should not marry or have children with African Americans was widespread in the North as well as the South in the 1800s. Wilmot titled his proposal "The White Man's Proviso," making it clear that, as he stated before Congress, "We wish to settle the territories with free white men."[2]

THE COMPROMISE OF 1850

In 1849, when California applied for admission to the Union, the slavery question exploded once again. South Carolina senator John C. Calhoun, the foremost defender of slavery, issued a warning: further Northern attempts to pass anything like the Wilmot Proviso for California would be met with serious resistance in his and other slave states.

Calhoun and a vocal group of extremists on both sides once again went into full battle mode, each side intent on sabotaging and undermining the positions of the other. Congress became virtually paralyzed over the subject of slavery. When the House reconvened after the election of President Zachary Taylor in 1849, it took three weeks of furious argument and 63 ballots before representatives could even elect a Speaker of the House of Representatives.[3] The nation watched anxiously, wondering how pro- and antislavery factions were ever going to agree on a variety of potentially explosive issues, not the least of which was what to do about California.

John C. Calhoun, a strong supporter of slavery, laid the groundwork for the United States to annex Texas during his time as a senator from South Carolina.

Despite the claims by Calhoun and others that no compromise was possible, more rational voices finally prevailed. Senators Henry Clay, Daniel Webster, and Stephen A. Douglas called for restraint and patience. They urged regional leaders to hold to civility, practical politics, and the traditional concepts of American unity embodied in the Constitution and Declaration of Independence. Once again it worked.

With the help of others, Henry Clay, "the Great Compromiser," brokered yet another deal, the Compromise of 1850. Essentially, the proposal offered concessions to both sides. It admitted California to the Union as a Free State and allowed the governments of any new states to decide for themselves whether they would be free or slave. At the same time, it banned slave trading, though not slavery itself, in Washington, DC. A final provision strengthened the Fugitive Slave Law, which had been introduced into the Constitution in 1787 as Article IV but never actively enforced. As rewritten after the 1850 Compromise, convicted violators of the law faced a fine of $1,000 and six months in jail.[4]

THE NASHVILLE CONVENTION

After the insult of the compromise, in June 1850, a group of Southern representatives gathered in Nashville, Tennessee. It was the first time in history that leaders from only slave states assembled in one place to discuss unified action. They discussed the possibility of leaving the Union if Congress did not grant them substantial protection for slavery. The governors of Mississippi and South Carolina had already begun arming militias.

The Compromise of 1850 was finalized in September 1850. It was intended to heal wounds and promote unity in the nation, but it had almost exactly the opposite effect. Though large majorities in both houses of Congress approved the proposal, both sides of the ongoing slave debate found much to dislike in the compromise.

Slave owners in the South were highly encouraged by the stronger Fugitive Slave Law, which gave them more power and motivation than ever before to pursue runaway slaves all the way to the Canadian border. But they also felt their rights as citizens were being violated, because slavery, so vital to their way of life, might be excluded from western territories when they applied for statehood. There were even angry threats of secession.

As for antislavery Northerners, they were happy over the stoppage of slave trading in the nation's capital and the admission of California as a Free State. But they were outraged at the stronger Fugitive Slave Law, which forced them to actively assist slave catchers in their despicable business. They warned Southerners threatening secession that breaking up the Union would never be accomplished without a fight—and they clearly did not mean a verbal one. "There is a higher law" than those made by men, New York Senator William H. Seward declared in Congress.[5] To many ears, the statement was shocking. Seward was bringing religion into the slavery argument. It was the kind of language routinely

TEXAS AND SLAVERY

Slavery in Texas was a touchy issue even before it became a state. The Mexican government encouraged Americans to settle there, and many did, including slave owners. But when Mexico abolished slavery in 1829, Texas slaveholders refused to accept it. The resulting clash eventually led to Texas independence and the Mexican-American War. The admission of Texas to the Union as a slave state only happened, after much drama and debate, in 1845.

used by impassioned abolitionists, not supposedly levelheaded congressmen.

But, in truth, Seward was only saying what many white Americans were also beginning to believe. The Compromise of 1850 had made slavery a personal matter of conscience for millions of whites who didn't own slaves. They had had little argument with slavery as long as it stayed in the South, but the compromise had brought the institution to Northern attention. It was an important shift in public opinion. A movement more powerful than Congress and the law had begun and would continue to gain strength in the coming decade.

The Fugitive Slave Law meant even if a slave escaped and made it to the North, capture was still possible.

CAUTION!
THE THREAT OF SLAVE CATCHERS

After the passage of the Fugitive Slave Law in 1850, many outraged people in Boston, Massachusetts, and other Northern cities defied the law by warning black citizens when slave catchers came to town. Kidnappings were not unheard of. One of the most famous of these was the capture of Solomon Northup, a free black man who was abducted in 1841 in Washington, DC, and taken to Louisiana by slave traders. He remained in slavery there until 1853, when friends and family members located him and obtained his release. Northup told his horrific story in a book, *Twelve Years a Slave*, which was made into an award-winning movie in 2013.

The sign at the right was written and posted in 1851 by abolitionist and Unitarian minister Reverend Theodore Parker, leader of the Boston Vigilance Committee. Members of the committee, made up of more than 200 people, black and white, were particularly outraged by the 1851 trial and return of escaped slave Thomas Sims to his former owners in Georgia.[6]

By 1854, four years after the Fugitive Slave Law had been passed, members of the Boston Vigilance Committee had successfully protected and aided 230 fugitive slaves.[7] At times, they took drastic measures to assist recaptured slaves. African-American member Lewis Hayden stormed into a courtroom and rescued fugitive slave Shadrach Minkins. Hayden then helped Minkins escape to Canada.

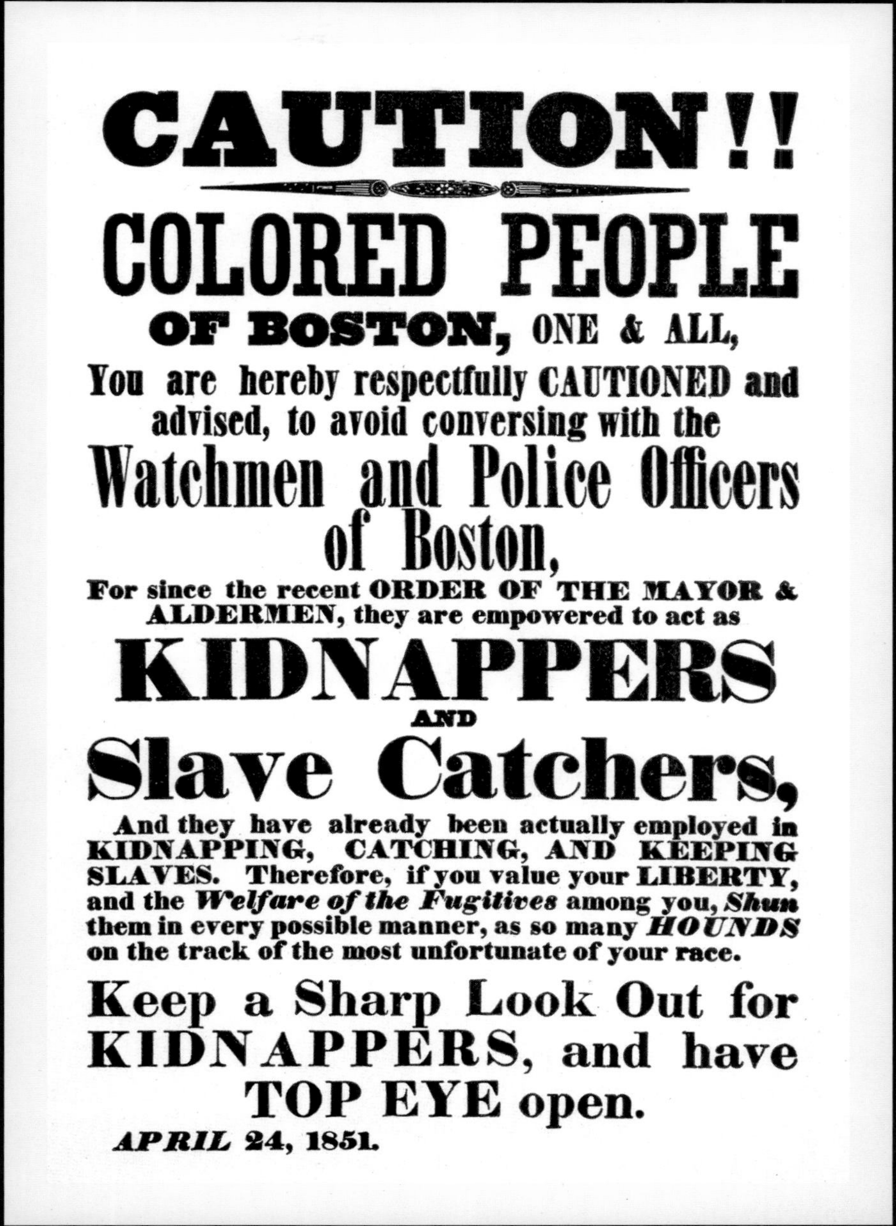

CAUTION!!

COLORED PEOPLE

OF BOSTON, ONE & ALL,

You are hereby respectfully CAUTIONED and advised, to avoid conversing with the

Watchmen and Police Officers of Boston,

For since the recent ORDER OF THE MAYOR & ALDERMEN, they are empowered to act as

KIDNAPPERS

AND

Slave Catchers,

And they have already been actually employed in KIDNAPPING, CATCHING, AND KEEPING SLAVES. Therefore, if you value your LIBERTY, and the *Welfare of the Fugitives* among you, *Shun* them in every possible manner, as so many *HOUNDS* on the track of the most unfortunate of your race.

Keep a Sharp Look Out for KIDNAPPERS, and have TOP EYE open.

***APRIL* 24, 1851.**

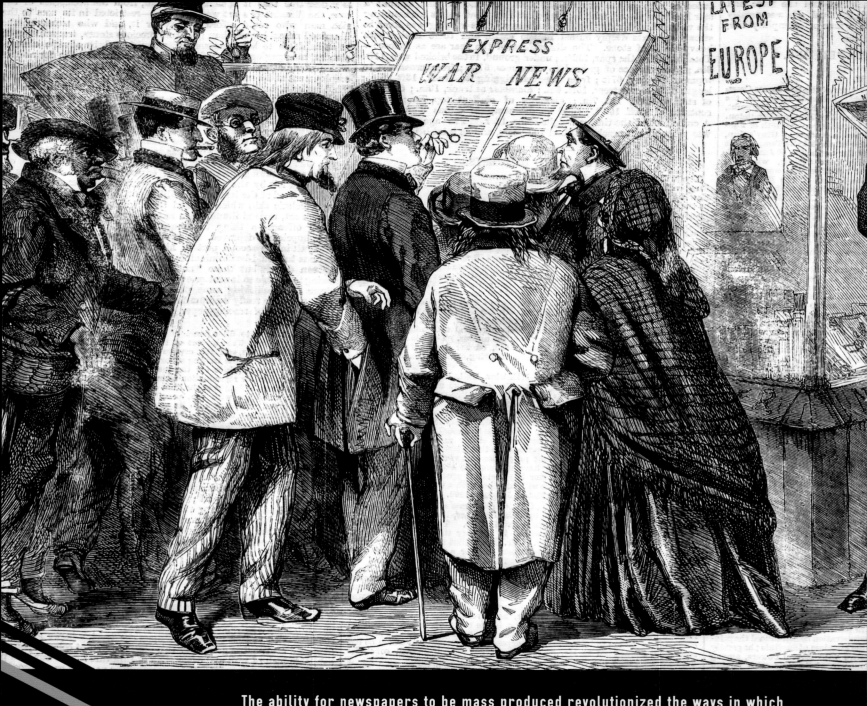

The ability for newspapers to be mass produced revolutionized the ways in which information spread.

NEW MEDIA AND PUBLIC OPINION

During the first four decades of the 1800s, people received information about what was happening in the rest of the nation slowly. Those who lived outside of major cities—most of the population—found out what was happening elsewhere mainly through letters or conversations with neighbors. Some received newspapers in the mail as well, but before 1840, newspapers were very different from how they are today. They carried a high volume of advertisements—including the entire front page—and each newspaper was affiliated with a political party. News articles were written from that party's perspective. These newspapers were also very expensive, costing approximately $10 for a year's subscription

THE SPREAD OF NEWSPAPERS

In 1840, the United States had only 1,404 newspapers, 138 of which were daily papers. By 1860, the nation had 3,725 newspapers, of which 387 were dailies. In the late 1850s, Philadelphia had a dozen daily papers. Chicago had 11, and Cincinnati and Saint Louis had 10 each.[3]

(approximately $280 in today's dollars).[1] Considering common laborers earned just seventy cents a day on average, only the wealthy could afford them.[2]

By the 1850s, though, a technological revolution in communications paved the way for modern newspapers. High-speed, steam-powered printing presses and the spread of railroads across the nation began to drastically cut the time it took for printed information to travel from one place to another. But it was the emergence of the telegraph around 1845 that quickly transformed news into an industry and created an explosion of daily newspapers.

Suddenly, descriptions of people and events could travel through wires strung in ever-expanding webs all across the country. Most large cities had multiple newspapers, and since they only cost a penny or two, nearly everybody could afford to buy one or more every day. Railroads and the US Postal Service carried millions of papers a day to rural areas as well.

The impact of newspapers on public opinion in the decade before the Civil War was immense. Newspapers of the 1850s not only printed the who, what, when, and where of the news but also the why. The concept of objective

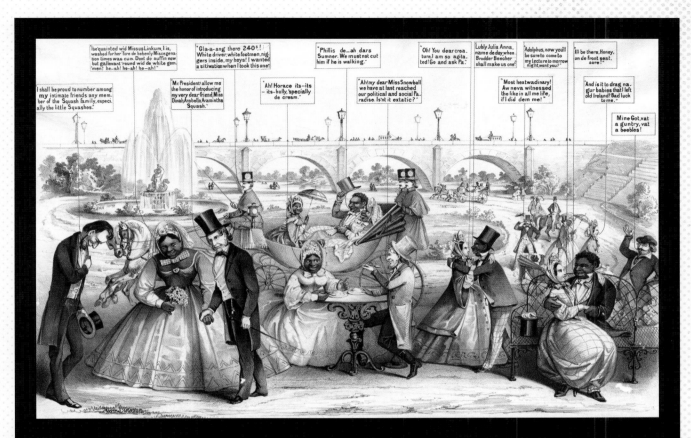

This proslavery propaganda cartoon suggests the end of slavery would lead to a mingling of the races and interracial marriage, which was considered taboo at the time.

reporting did not exist as it does today. Newspapers took sides on issues and told readers what they should think. To sell more papers, most publishers adopted a sensational style and approach, attempting to whip local sentiments into a frenzy for or against specific causes and issues. In this way, daily newspapers flourished and became important controllers and molders of public opinion.

Mail service and railroads in the rural South were far less widespread or efficient than in the more urban North. This fact alone may explain why news did not reach as far or as quickly into Southern states as it did in Northern ones. This does not mean Southerners didn't read newspapers. There were many available, though far fewer than in the North. While propaganda was prevalent throughout the nation, the slow movement of information in the South may have given publishers an advantage in controlling what readers read—and therefore what they believed. Newspapers fueled Southern support by printing articles that insisted the Confederate cause was not just about slavery—it was a matter of freedom and independence. This propaganda would continue after the war had begun. A Richmond newspaper declared, "'The people of the South,' says a contemporary, 'are not fighting for slavery but for independence,'" and went on to explain that, "Our doctrine is this: WE ARE FIGHTING FOR INDEPENDENCE THAT OUR GREAT AND NECESSARY DOMESTIC INSTITUTION OF SLAVERY SHALL BE PRESERVED, and for the preservation of other institutions of which slavery is the groundwork."[4]

As the railroad expanded and pushed into new territories, newspapers were

DEFENDERS OF SLAVERY

Southern slavery supporters pointed out the end of slavery would result in a lack of field hands, which would lead to the instant collapse of the Southern economy and ruination of cotton, tobacco, and rice crops if emancipation were enacted. They further argued the immediate release of all slaves would end in a mass chaos of unemployed and homeless people.

Slavery had existed for centuries, and defenders of slavery argued it was the natural order of things. The Greeks and Romans kept slaves, and so had the English. They said the Bible accepted slavery, highlighting that Abraham of the Old Testament had owned slaves. They further argued the Ten Commandments instructed the Jews not to covet, or wish to possess, their neighbors' servants.

Slavery was, in the minds of its proponents, a divine institution that had introduced Africans to Christianity. Calhoun spoke in support of slavery, declaring, "Never before has the black race of Central Africa, from the dawn of history to the present day, attained a condition so civilized and so improved, not only physically, but morally and intellectually."[5]

ABOLITIONISTS

Abolitionists attempted to control public opinion, too. Early antislavery groups were composed mainly of religious groups that opposed slavery. One of these was the Quakers. The Quakers were a Christian group who refused to participate in war, abstained from alcohol, and committed themselves to living a simple and devout life. They were some of the first to question the morality of slavery. They established committees and petitioned British Parliament in the 1780s to put an end to the slave trade.

FIRE-EATERS

The counterparts of abolitionists in the North were "fire-eaters" in the South. These fiery secessionists engaged in loud, negative propaganda. In the 1850s, they were viewed as fanatical and dangerous, even in the South. Their secessionist language often drowned out saner, calmer voices. This gave Northerners the false impression that everyone in the South was in favor of disunion.

These early abolitionists were eventually joined by some Baptists and Methodists who also disagreed with slavery based on a deep religious conviction. Others began joining the movement, and by the 1830s, the antislavery movement included other Christian groups, freed slaves, and many women. They became active and outspoken in their beliefs. The American Anti-Slavery movement was the largest organized abolitionist group, with more than 250,000 members before the war.[6]

One underlying belief on the part of abolitionists was that the South was determined to bring the Northern states under political control, in much the same way as slaveholders controlled their slaves. The result was a pervasive Northern belief in a highly organized Southern conspiracy, or "Slave Power."[7] At the same time, the South was also coming to believe the same thing about the North. A perception arose that everyone in the North was just as shrill and fanatical as Southerners thought abolitionists were.

However, the North was by no means unified on the issue of slavery. For decades before the war, abolitionists such as William Lloyd Garrison were as despised in the North as they were in the South. Similar to most Southerners in the 1830s and 1840s, most Americans in the North were racially prejudiced. But since approximately 95 percent of all blacks in the nation were in the South, most people in the North were happy to let things be, so long as slavery stayed where it was.[8] Garrison and other abolitionists, who wanted to free all slaves, were generally seen as troublemakers and serious threats to the peace and harmony of the nation. Supporters of slavery feared Garrison sought to flood the nation with black people. Certainly in the South, people were convinced he was determined to start an all-out race war and held him personally responsible for slave insurrections.

ATTACKING ABOLITIONISTS

William Lloyd Garrison and other abolitionists were frequently attacked by angry mobs when they spoke. Garrison was once almost hanged by protestors in Boston. Abolitionist editor Elijah P. Lovejoy dared to confront slaveholders on their territory and paid a heavy price. He was attacked and killed by an angry mob in Missouri. For years, newspapers printed sensational accounts of such incidents, more often backing the attackers and opposing the free speech claims of abolitionists.

WILLIAM LLOYD GARRISON

1805–1879

Perhaps the most vocal abolitionist was Massachusetts-born William Lloyd Garrison. Convinced that God had recruited him to actively combat slavery, he became a leading, though controversial, figure in the movement. Through his monthly newspaper, the *Liberator*, Garrison pushed an uncompromising message of total and immediate emancipation of the slaves. His belief that "nothing but extensive revivals of pure religion can save our country" was similar to what other abolitionists were saying.[9] But Garrison's extremism set him apart. His tone and language were much more strident and graphic, depicting slavery as a violent crime perpetrated by vicious, unfeeling degenerates.

Though his paper had only a few subscribers, Garrison mailed copies to newspapers all over the North and South. Southern editors routinely reprinted Garrison's rants against slavery, slaveholders, and Southerners in general. Over time, Southerners formed the impression that all Northerners were as fanatical as Garrison and other abolitionists.

In June 1840, more than 500 abolitionists met at the General Anti-Slavery Convention in London, England, to discuss slavery.

John Brown's raid on Harpers Ferry helped push the nation closer to Civil War.

In truth, abolitionists in the mid-1800s were a small and unpopular minority. They were also divided. Some abolitionists wanted slavery to be illegal only in new states. Others were more radical, calling for the immediate emancipation of slaves in every state. These abolitionists were very vocal about the need for slavery to end. Garrison went so far as to publicly burn a copy of the

Constitution, which he called a pact with the devil because it allowed slavery. Such extreme acts outraged many people, but they also spurred some into action.

On the night of October 16, 1859, 20 armed men snuck quietly into the unsuspecting Virginia town of Harpers Ferry. They quickly overpowered a guard and took possession of a US Army arsenal and rifle factory. Leading the force was John Brown, a fanatically religious abolitionist who believed slavery was a sin and that God had appointed him to end it. His plan was to use the vast stockpile at Harpers Ferry to supply an army of slaves with the weapons they needed to wage bloody war against white slave owners in the South.

It was not to be. Federal troops quickly surrounded and killed most of the insurgents. Brown was captured, which may have been his plan all along. Shortly before his public execution, he wrote: "I am . . . now quite certain that the great crime of this guilty land will never be purged away but with blood."[10] Church bells pealed across New England, where Brown was generally hailed as a martyr. Many black people, free and slave, hailed him as a saint. Most white Americans, however, saw Brown as a prime example of what can happen when fanaticism overpowers rational thoughts and actions.

John Brown, *center*, was captured and sentenced to hang for treason, murder, and insurrection.

Representative Brooks's assault on Senator Sumner demonstrated how torn the nation was becoming over slavery.

BLEEDING KANSAS: THE WIDENING GULF

The Senate chamber in Washington, DC, was quiet and nearly empty on May 22, 1856. The morning session had adjourned, and only a few members remained. One of them, Senator Charles Sumner, sat at his desk quietly working when Preston Brooks, a member of the House of Representatives, approached.

"You have libeled my state and slandered my relation," Brooks said. "And I feel it to be my duty to punish you for it."[1] He lifted a heavy, metal-capped walking stick and began beating Sumner repeatedly across the head and body. Sumner tried vainly to escape and finally fell to the floor, unconscious. Brooks continued the attack until his cane shattered.

The insult Brooks referred to was made in a speech Sumner gave a few days earlier. The speech, entitled "The Crime against Kansas," expressed the senator's (and many Northerners') intense feelings over events in the newly formed state, where disagreements between pro- and antislavery settlers had erupted into bloody fighting. Those expressions were not as objectionable, however, as the crude and vulgar comments Sumner also inserted about Brooks's home state of South Carolina and his cousin, Senator Andrew P. Butler. Those remarks had deeply offended Brooks's sense of honor, and he felt obligated to get revenge.

THE CANING OF SENATOR SUMNER

Congressman Preston Brooks was never charged with any crime for his assault on Charles Sumner. He did resign his seat in the House, however, and subsequently received dozens of new canes as gifts from admiring Southerners. Sumner never fully recovered from his injuries, though he did return to the Senate four years later. His Massachusetts constituents kept his seat open all that time in his support and in protest of Southern brutality.

Such a brutal attack in the Capitol revealed for many people just how bitter and personal the conflict between North and South had become in a few short years. The incident also illustrated the extent to which recent events in Kansas had driven a wedge into the heart of the nation and how wide the resulting split was growing.

BLEEDING KANSAS

By 1854, the South had long since lost its majority in the House of Representatives, though Southerners still maintained their share of power in the Senate. More and more, Southern states recognized their last real hope of regaining control of the government and their own fate lay in spreading slavery to territories and states in the West.

Their hopes were bolstered by Democratic senator Stephen A. Douglas of Illinois, a firm believer in the principle of popular sovereignty. This was the concept that residents of new states should have the right to decide for themselves whether their state would be free or slave. So, when Douglas introduced a bill in Congress on January 4, 1854, that would divide the Nebraska Territory into two new states, Nebraska and Kansas, he added the popular sovereignty provision. Northerners were outraged. Yet, despite their protests, the Kansas-Nebraska Act passed. The result was a situation that essentially repealed the Missouri Compromise of 1820 by allowing any state, even those north of the thirty-sixth parallel, to become a slave state if residents voted that way.

Implied in Douglas's sponsorship of the bill was the expectation that, since Kansas bordered the slave state of Missouri, it would become a slave state and

Armed Missourians, called border ruffians, poured into Kansas to fraudulently

Nebraska would become a Free State. Of course, in 1855, nothing was assured. Residents still had to vote.

On election day in 1856, chaos ensued in Kansas. More than 1,000 armed, proslavery residents of Missouri poured across Kansas's borders.[2] They fraudulently cast thousands of votes and elected a legislature composed exclusively of proslavery men. Determined Free-Soil settlers, or settlers who moved into the Free State territory to claim free soil for white farmers, were certain the federal government would quickly recognize the treachery and evict the intruders. They formed their own government, which was based on their conviction that Manifest Destiny meant land for free whites, not white-owned blacks.

Bloody skirmishes broke out between proslavery settlers and free-staters. Shootings, stabbings, and mob violence quickly turned the territory into a battleground. In the spring of 1856, Missourians attacked and burned the town of Lawrence, Kansas. New York publisher Horace Greely coined the phrase

THE KANSAS DEBACLE

In 1857, in an effort to end the bloodshed in Kansas, President James Buchanan arranged for another vote to determine residents' wishes concerning slavery. But, once again, free political procedure was hijacked by proslave ruffians, who formed a convention that adopted a fraudulent proslave constitution. At the same time, legitimate Kansas voters held their own election and overwhelmingly rejected statehood and the fraudulent constitution. After years of wrangling, Kansas was finally admitted to the Union in 1861 as a Free State.

The Kansas-Nebraska Act allowed residents of territories to vote whether their state would be free or slave, which prompted riots in Kansas.

"Bleeding Kansas" to describe the bitter fighting that claimed the lives of more than 200 people in only three months that year.[3]

One side effect of the Kansas-Nebraska Act was the splintering of former political parties into dozens of factions. Out of the chaos soon formed two opposing political parties. The Democrats remained as they formerly were—mostly southern and proslavery. The other, the Republicans, was a completely new party made up of former Whigs and other factions united by their mutual opposition to the extension of slavery. As the "Free-Soil Party," Republicans vowed to "engage in competition for the virgin soil of Kansas."[4]

DRED SCOTT

In 1857, while the battle over slavery still raged in Kansas, the US Supreme Court handed down a ruling on a case that made matters even worse. It involved an enslaved man named Dred Scott. Since 1830, Scott had lived in Illinois and Wisconsin, both Free States, with his owner. When his owner died in 1843, Scott attempted to buy his freedom, but the owner's family refused. Scott sued, claiming his long residency in Free States entitled him to freedom.

Millions watched the case with interest as it made its way through various courts of appeal without resolution. At the heart of the matter, after all, were issues that divided the nation: Who had the power to decide whether Western states were free or slave? What was the legal status of blacks in the United States?

The case finally landed in the Supreme Court, one place where Southern political power still held sway. Five of the nine justices were Southern Democrats.[5] Chief Justice Roger B. Taney of Maryland had long feared the slavery issue might tear apart the Union. He had expressed hope the Supreme Court would get an opportunity to put the divisive issue to rest once and for all. The *Dred Scott* case appeared to be that opportunity.

Unfortunately, the majority decision read by Taney on March 6, 1857, did nothing to calm the storm raging over the slavery issue. The court ruled that according to the Constitution, slaves had no rights to citizenship or anything else. They were property, not people, in the eyes of the law. Black persons, it said, must be "regarded as beings of an inferior order, and altogether unfit to associate with the white race . . . so far inferior that they have no rights which the white man is bound to respect."[6] Therefore, it concluded, "the negro might justly and lawfully be reduced to slavery for his benefit."[7] The ruling went even further. It also ruled that prior acts of Congress excluding slavery from new states and territories were unconstitutional.

The *Dred Scott* ruling was devastating for many Americans, even those with no previous abolitionist sentiments. It confirmed and added to the general paranoia in Northern states over a Slave Power conspiracy in high places in the government. Worse, the ruling essentially negated congressional authority and all previous compromises concerning where slavery could exist. It meant anyone

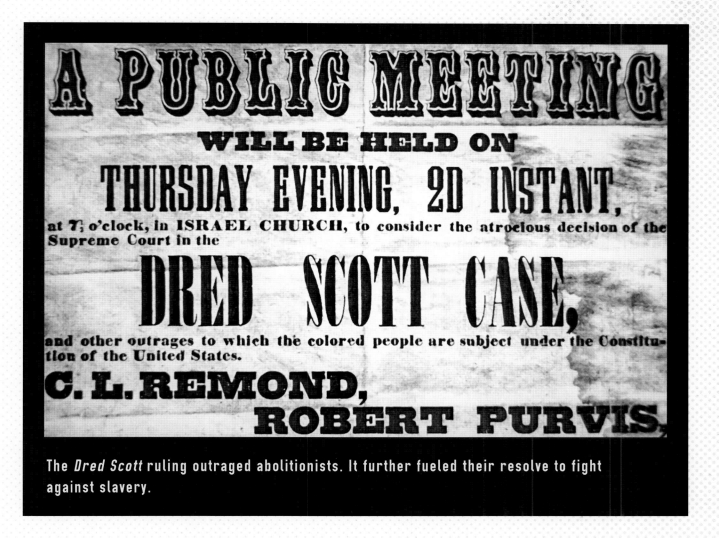

A PUBLIC MEETING

WILL BE HELD ON

THURSDAY EVENING, 2D INSTANT,

at 7½ o'clock, in ISRAEL CHURCH, to consider the atrocious decision of the Supreme Court in the

DRED SCOTT CASE,

and other outrages to which the colored people are subject under the Constitution of the United States.

C. L. REMOND,
ROBERT PURVIS,

The *Dred Scott* ruling outraged abolitionists. It further fueled their resolve to fight against slavery.

(including slaver owners) could legally take their property (including slaves) to any state of the Union. The court's specifically racist language was especially troubling for tens of thousands of free black people, especially those in the

South. It effectively removed their rights and made them vulnerable to capture and enslavement despite their free status.

Proslavery Southerners celebrated the ruling, which supported everything they believed and stood for. Free-Soilers and abolitionists were stunned but defiant, vowing to never obey any ruling that obviously violated the rights of so many Americans. Legislators in Washington were bewildered. What about the Missouri Compromise and the Compromise of 1850? Did Congress have any say at all over what happened in the territories?

In that confusing and bitter atmosphere, Congress met on February 6, 1858, to debate the continuing standoff in Kansas. The state, still wracked by fraud and violence, was in turmoil. Something had to done, but what? Frustrations grew and nerves quickly frayed as members of both houses tried to sort things

WOMEN'S RIGHTS AND ABOLITION

The beginning of the women's rights movement was closely connected to the abolition movement in the United States. The first women's rights convention, held in 1848 at Seneca Falls, New York, was organized by feminist abolitionists Lucretia Mott and Elizabeth Cady Stanton. Their "Declaration of Rights and Sentiments," presented there for the first time, advocated voting rights for women.[8] Many of the attendees also supported the emancipation of slaves. Frederick Douglass, who attended the convention, enthusiastically supported the movement. But many Northern and Southern men thought feminists were unnatural monsters. As one writer said, "They have no heart, no sympathy, no reason, no conscience."[9]

out. During one session in the House, tempers flared. A South Carolina representative and a congressman from Pennsylvania got into a heated argument and finally lunged at one another. Within minutes, a fight broke out involving some 50 congressmen, punching, tackling, and screaming insults while the Speaker vainly called for order.[10]

In a speech that year, William H. Seward, a senator from New York, spoke with deep conviction to an audience of like-minded Republicans. He spoke about the two separate and very different political parties in the nation. One was the Democratic Party, based on slavery and inequality. The other was

A debate about slavery resulted in the most infamous brawl in the history of the US House of Representatives on February 6, 1858.

FRANK LESLIE'S ILLUSTRATED NEWSPAPER

Entered according to Act of Congress in the year 1857, by FRANK LESLIE, in the Clerk's Office of the District Court for the Southern District of New York. (Copyrighted February 15, 1858.)

No. 116.—Vol. V.] NEW YORK, SATURDAY, FEBRUARY 20, 1858. [PRICE 6 CENTS

CONTENTS.

THE CONGRESSIONAL ROW.

On Friday night, in the year of our Lord eighteen hundred and fifty-eight, and the morning of Saturday, which was February sixth, before cock crowing, and yet after midnight, just about the time, according to poetical authority, that graveyards yawn, the United States House of Representatives was the scene of a spirited discussion on the "State of the Union." The members of that "deliberative body," who are generally as averse to any useful employment as New York policemen are to temperance practices, and who for the ostensible object of business generally assemble in the middle of the day, for the want of something better to do on the occasion referred to, concluded, in place of the futile experiment of exercising their brains, that they would test their physical endurance, and see who could keep out of bed the longest. The contest was very interesting "to outsiders," and presented a scene, which, for all that is lamentable in human nature and our national fame, was, even for a Washington city row, pre-eminently disgusting.

The members exhibited towards the close of the careful struggle some curious pictures; some were doubled up and others doubled down. The "Western delegates" usually hung on backs of their chairs, displaying open mouths and giving utterance to dreadful sounds; they had learned this attitude and expression in the wayside groggeries. The "Eastern men," in their slumber assumed reverential attitudes, and seemed to be lost in devotional exercise. The "chivalry" seemed to be restive and fighting mosquitoes, and they were, therefore, the widest of any of their fellow-sufferers. Speaker Orr maintained dignified good-nature, and though lost to "outward things," his right arm mechanically brought down his gavel upon his [table] him unintentionally but truthfully indicating that the body was continually "out of order." The clerks, whose business it was to call the "yeas and nays," first gabbled at their desks like so many geese, then became less articulate, and finally their "herculean task," broke down altogether. The news reporters in the side galleries, under the delusion that they were in a vast oyster saloon in a state of drunken demoralization, took to cracking smutty jokes and pelting each other with spit-[balls]

CONGRESSIONAL ROW, IN THE U. S. HOUSE OF REPRESENTATIVES, MIDNIGHT OF FRIDAY, FEBRUARY 5TH, 1858.

the Republican Party, based on the concept of freedom and equality. "It is an irrepressible conflict between opposing and enduring forces," he said. "And it means that the United States must and will, sooner or later, become either entirely a slave-holding nation, or entirely a free-labor nation."[11] The time was rapidly approaching for an "inevitable collision" between these two forces, he said, because compromise was now no longer possible.[12]

Southerners did not radically disagree with Seward's appraisal of the situation—only with his assessment of which side was the real enemy of freedom and justice. They believed their ideas of slavery and revolution put them closest to the intentions the Founding Fathers expressed in the Constitution and Declaration of Independence.

Each side based its position on religious principles. Both North and South had reached the dangerous point where compromise meant submitting to the enemy.

HARRIET BEECHER STOWE

1811–1896

Harriet Beecher Stowe was the daughter of Lyman Beecher, a prominent minister whose brother was abolitionist Henry Ward Beecher. As a girl, Harriet came to share her uncle's conviction that slavery was a national sin God would not long tolerate. Later, when her first child died suddenly, she sought a way to divert her mind and ease her grief. She decided to write a book about the evils of slavery.

When it appeared in the spring of 1852, *Uncle Tom's Cabin* took the nation by storm. It sold 300,000 copies before the end of the year and kept selling for years thereafter.[13] The book's depiction of slaves as human beings, with the same feelings and hopes as white people, was an epiphany for millions of readers. So was her message that Northerners, by their acceptance of slavery, were as guilty in the eyes of God as any brutal Southern slave-beater. *Uncle Tom's Cabin* did not start the Civil War, as some have claimed. But it did much to change Northern attitudes about African Americans and slavery.

Abraham Lincoln was not well-known outside the state of Illinois when he

THE RISE OF LINCOLN

The *Dred Scott* ruling outraged many in the North, leading some to oppose the decision in every way possible. At the same time, a new and intense wave of religious fervor swept the Northeast and Midwest in 1857 and 1858.

Perhaps it was a reaction to spreading violence. Or it may have stemmed from the bad economic times that had descended on the nation due to a crash in the commercial railroad industry, which caused many businesses to go under. Likely, it was simply an attempt by middle-class Americans to return to what they saw as

America's fundamental values. Whatever the reason, the religious revival altered many people's perceptions of the nation and its future.

Newspapers called it "the Great Revival."[1] In the late 1850s, many Americans began to see national events and crises as part of a higher plan in which they were destined to play an important role. Politics offered a way to participate in that plan, and for many Northerners, the Republican Party was the best representation of the Christian values they were seeking. During the election of 1856, the Republican Party's presidential convention took on a religiously charged tone. Republicans made a point of disassociating their principles from those of abolitionists, still seen by most Americans as fanatics. Still, their platform was strongly antislavery. Preserving the Union and the basic ideals of the Founding Fathers were equally important. Certainly, according to many Northern Republicans, nothing was more incompatible with those ideals than slavery. Republicans believed the United States was a beacon for freedom and justice in the world, and it could not shine with a pure light so long as the institution of human bondage existed in the nation.

Democrats, too, revered the Union and Christianity, but their perception of those things was fundamentally different from that of Republicans. Democrats believed the Union was largely founded by slave owners who valued the institution and understood its worth. The nation they created was an equal partnership between Free States and slave states. That agreement, which they believed God had ordained and perpetuated, had lasted 80 years, and it remained a sacred contract. Any attempt to break that agreement was a reproach to the Founding Fathers and Heaven.

Into this heightened religious and political atmosphere stepped a new and unique national figure. In 1858, Abraham Lincoln was well-known and liked in Illinois, where he had practiced law and local politics for years. In other parts of the country, though, his sudden appearance in national politics came as a surprise to many. It took a while for people to recognize that behind his rough appearance and backwoods manner was a razor-sharp intellect and abiding reverence for freedom and the Union.

Lincoln's rise to political prominence coincided with the rise of the Republican Party. Its principles of opposing the extension of slavery and Southern disunion meshed perfectly with his personal convictions. But Lincoln, seeming to read the mood of America, took it a step further. During debates against Stephen A. Douglas in the 1857–1858 campaign for an

THE LINCOLN—DOUGLAS DEBATES

Abraham Lincoln and Stephen A. Douglas met in seven dramatic debates in 1858 during the campaign for one of Illinois's two US Senate seats. At the time, Lincoln was largely unknown outside of Illinois. Douglas, however, was a national celebrity, so the debates generated intense interest across the nation. Newspapers sent people to transcribe the candidates' speeches, which appeared in newspapers only hours later. In that way, Lincoln's name and ideas spread quickly. When he lost that local election, Lincoln thought his political career was over. But nationwide publicity saved him. The next time he and Douglas faced off was in the 1860 presidential race, with a much different outcome.

Illinois Senate seat, Lincoln sometimes tinged his oratory with religious imagery and biblical references, but his main argument against slavery rested upon the affirmation in the Declaration of Independence that "all men are created equal."[2]

THE MOCKING OF A CANDIDATE

Lincoln's opponents made fun of his limited experience as a political leader and his backwoods style every chance they got. A favorite subject of ridicule was his gangly appearance, implying that Lincoln's craggy face and lanky frame would be an embarrassment to the nation. Many attacks were racist. One claimed that Lincoln's election would foster interracial marriage, while another claimed that if Lincoln was elected, in "ten years or less our children will be the slaves of Negroes."[3]

LINCOLN FOR PRESIDENT

Lincoln did not win the 1858 Senate race, but he drew considerable attention from prominent Republicans in the East. In 1860 the Republican Party convention at Chicago nominated him for the presidency. Running against him were candidates nominated by various factions of a splintered Democratic Party—John C. Breckinridge of the Southern Democratic Party and Stephen A. Douglas of the Northern Democratic Party—as well as John Bell of the Constitutional Union Party. Southerners could not agree on a favorite, but they did agree on who must not win. Slave-state leaders warned a Republican victory in the 1860 election spelled the end of the Union.

The presidential campaign of 1860 was strangely calm for Lincoln. Between the time he was nominated and the election in November, he did very little actual campaigning. At that time it was considered undignified for presidential candidates to travel to rallies and events. Other prominent Republicans did a great deal of speaking for him, but Lincoln stayed in Illinois.

Wide support of the Republican platform in the North, as well as the splintering of the Democratic Party, helped give Lincoln the presidency. He won the election with almost no Southern votes. He was not even on the ballot in ten Southern slave states. Though he got less than a majority of the popular vote, he had a solid majority in the Electoral

Political cartoons often poked fun at Lincoln's tall stature.

THE UNION MUST AND

SHALL BE PRESERVED

FREE SPEECH,
FREE HOMES,
FREE TERRITORY.

PROTECTION
TO
AMERICAN
INDUSTRY

FOR PRESIDENT
ABRAHAM LINCOLN
OF ILLINOIS

FOR VICE PRESIDENT
HANNIBAL HAMLIN
OF MAINE

preserving

College, and was elected president on November 6, 1860.

After the election, many people in the South who had hoped for a compromise to avoid secession changed their minds. Fire-eaters renewed their agitation for immediate and total separation of slave states from the Union. To them, it was clear: whatever power the South might have had to control the national government was gone. Lincoln's election was the last straw. Only one option was open for them now: secession.

LINCOLN AT COOPER UNION

In late 1859, Lincoln was invited to give a speech at the Cooper Union Institute in New York City. Although it is not well remembered today, that speech proved to be perhaps the most important speech of Lincoln's political career. Lincoln set out to prove the Founding Fathers had intended Congress to regulate slavery. This was the exact opposite of the conclusion reached in Supreme Court justice Roger Taney's ruling in the *Dred Scott* case. The speech was a complete triumph and, thanks largely to New York newspapers that reported on the event, Lincoln became an overnight political star.

PHOTO OF ABRAHAM LINCOLN
MATHEW BRADY'S PORTRAIT

Mathew Brady photographed presidential candidate Abraham Lincoln on February 27, 1860, hours before Lincoln addressed an enthusiastic audience at Cooper Union Institute in New York. Photography had only existed since around 1839, but Lincoln understood early on the power of the new technology. Even before his presidential campaign, he used pictures to show people the kind of person he really was. Brady did that too. That's why he decided to photograph Lincoln standing, to accentuate his unusual height. He also posed him with his hand on a stack of books to suggest his education and intelligence. One thing Brady did hide, though, was Lincoln's long, scrawny neck. He pulled Lincoln's collar up to hide it before he took the picture. Lincoln liked the photo. It was reprinted dozens of times in newspapers and magazines, and it worked. Many Americans formed their first favorable opinion of Lincoln based on that picture.

Lincoln credited Brady with helping him win the presidency, stating, "Brady and the Cooper Union speech made me president of the United States . . . [the photograph] dispelled the opposition based on the rumors of my long ungainly figure, large feet, clumsy hands, and long, gaunt head; making me into a man of human aspect and dignified bearing."[4]

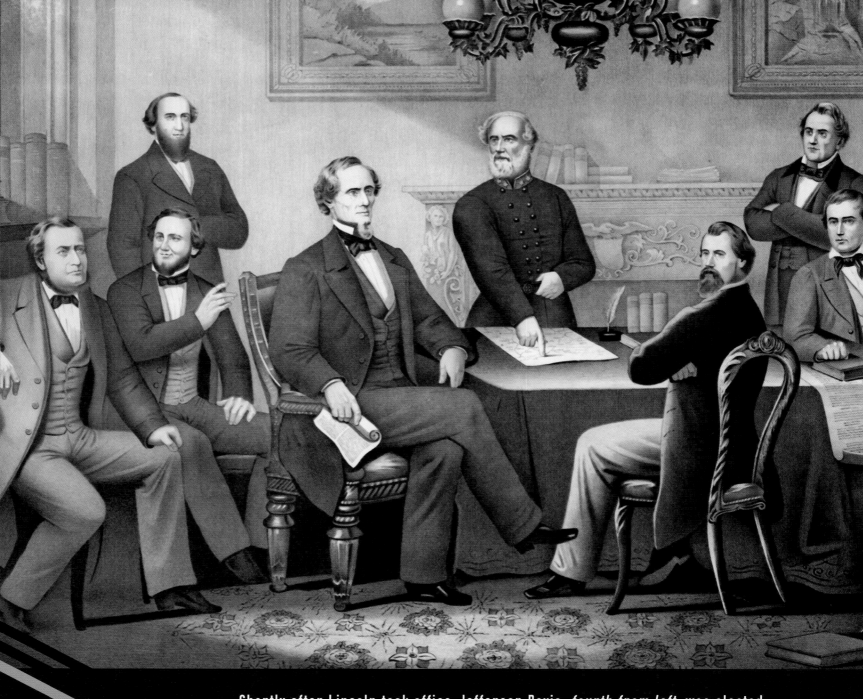

Shortly after Lincoln took office, Jefferson Davis, *fourth from left*, was elected president of the Confederate States of America.

"NO COMPROMISE!"

With the nation on the brink of war, desperate people still made last-ditch efforts to delay the inevitable. In December 1860, Senator John J. Crittenden of Kentucky proposed a compromise. Nearly all aspects of his proposal attempted to soothe the South while offering almost nothing to the North. Crittenden's proposal called for a line along the 36°30' latitude all the way from the Ohio River to the Pacific Ocean, south of which all states would be slave states. Besides that, Crittenden offered to put a clause in the Constitution stating Congress would pay the owners of escaped slaves for their losses and never again interfere with interstate slave trade, and never attempt to abolish slavery anywhere in the nation. Not surprisingly, Northern states refused to even consider such a plan.

A compromise plan offered in January 1861 by the man Lincoln had selected to appoint to the position of secretary of state, William Seward, proposed many of the same things. But it also included laws that would prevent states from invading one another and repeal ordinances in Northern states against returning fugitive slaves to their owners. Seceded states, which included South Carolina, Mississippi, Florida, Alabama, Georgia, Louisiana, and Texas, boycotted a Peace Convention that met in February 1861, so it ultimately served no practical purpose. In that same month, Jefferson Davis made a speech after being elected the president of the Confederate States of America, making the South's position very clear: "No compromise, no reconstruction [of the Union]," he said, "can now be entertained."[1]

Washington, DC, was dreary, cold, and windy on March 4, 1861, Lincoln's inauguration day. At least 25,000 people gathered in front of the Capitol Building to see the new president.[2] Many, no doubt, gazing at the half-completed dome and piles of lumber and stone around the area, recognized the still-unfinished Capitol as a symbol of the nation itself—still in pieces, waiting to be assembled. What could the president possibly say or do now, people must have wondered, to help make that happen?

Washington, DC, was like an armed camp. The simmering situation in the South and threats of violence from all sides prompted an unprecedented show of force everywhere along the president's parade route and at the Capitol.

In the North, thousands turned out for Lincoln's inauguration. His election moved the South closer to war.

Armed soldiers roamed the streets, and sharpshooters took positions at open windows and on the roof overlooking the presentation platform, fluttering with red, white, and blue bunting. Lincoln looked grim and nervous while he waited to take the oath of office and deliver his inaugural address.

Lincoln's tentative manner changed when he spoke. His voice was clear and strong. He first sought to reassure a frightened North that civil war did not have to happen, and he doubted it would. He told the South he did not intend to halt slavery there, but he also declared that he did not intend to allow them to dissolve the Union, either. And, to make his point clear, he addressed Southerners directly. "In your hands, my dissatisfied fellow-countrymen, and not in mine, is the momentous issue of civil war."[3] He had sworn an oath, he said, to "preserve, protect, and defend" the Constitution and the United States of America, and that is what he intended to do.[4]

THE CORWIN COMPROMISE

Both houses of Congress accepted a last-minute compromise by Ohio Senator Thomas Corwin the day before Lincoln's inauguration. Corwin's proposal was simple: a constitutional amendment, the thirteenth, which would forever block Congress from interfering with slavery in any state that already had it. Lincoln even mentioned the proposal in his first inaugural address and called for states to ratify it. But once the war started, Lincoln changed his mind. Emancipation of slaves, not the perpetual continuation of slavery, was the purpose of the Thirteenth Amendment when it was finally passed in 1865.

LINCOLN'S DILEMMA

The day after he was inaugurated, Lincoln was presented with one of the greatest crises in American history. He received an urgent message from Major Robert Anderson informing him that supplies at Fort Sumter were running dangerously low. If food did not arrive in six weeks, Anderson said, he and his men would be forced to surrender.

The dilemma, as Lincoln saw it, involved two options. He could order Anderson to surrender Fort Sumter, as many people were advising him to do. This would delay war, certainly. But Lincoln had vowed during his campaign and inaugural address that he intended to "hold, occupy, and possess the property and places belonging to the government."[6] He did not feel he could go back on the pledge now by simply giving Sumter to the South Carolina Militia. Giving in also meant he recognized their sovereignty—the Confederate states' right to exist as a separate entity from the Union. That went against his every instinct and belief, and he could not in good conscience send that message. The other option was no better. He could send warships to resupply the fort, but that would mean they would have to go into Charleston Harbor with guns blazing. He had declared repeatedly that if war came, it would not be because the US government fired the first shot.

As he pondered his choices, Lincoln realized he had a third option, and he devised a clever plan. He sent a message to Confederate president Davis, advising him of his intention to send a fleet of warships to accompany a supply boat that would carry food and nothing else to Fort Sumter. The warships would not attack or enter Charleston Harbor unless the supply boat was fired upon. If rebel artillery fired, however, the warships would attack, and war would begin. Lincoln's plan essentially placed the choice of whether to start the war in Davis's hands, not his. Davis, believing it was time to assert the South's authority, took the bait and gave the order to attack.

On the morning of April 12, the bombardment of Fort Sumter began and lasted for 33 straight hours. Jubilant Charlestonians flocked to the harbor and gathered on rooftops to watch the fireworks show. Inside Sumter, Major Anderson and his men huddled in sturdy stone fortifications and fired back,

Charleston residents watched from rooftops as Confederate troops bombarded

while more than 4,000 shells exploded into or over the fort.[7] At noon the following day, with fires raging out of control and ammunition and supplies almost gone, Anderson surrendered. He and his men were allowed to leave the next day. They ceremonially saluted their shell-tattered flag as it was lowered and took it with them when they marched to boats waiting to take them north to safety. Incredibly, not a single man on either side was killed by enemy fire in the battle that officially began the bloodiest war in American history.

WHO FIRED THE FIRST SHOT?

History books name Edmund Ruffin as the individual who fired the first shot at Sumter the morning of April 12. A rabid fire-eater, Ruffin reportedly said later, "Of course, I was gratified by the compliment, and delighted to perform the service."[8] In truth, though, Ruffin fired the second shot, not the first. That mortar shell was launched at precisely 4:30 a.m. by order of General Beauregard, commander of rebel artillery installations, as a signal for the attack to begin.

Major Anderson and his men valiantly defended Fort Sumter against the rebels' bombardment.

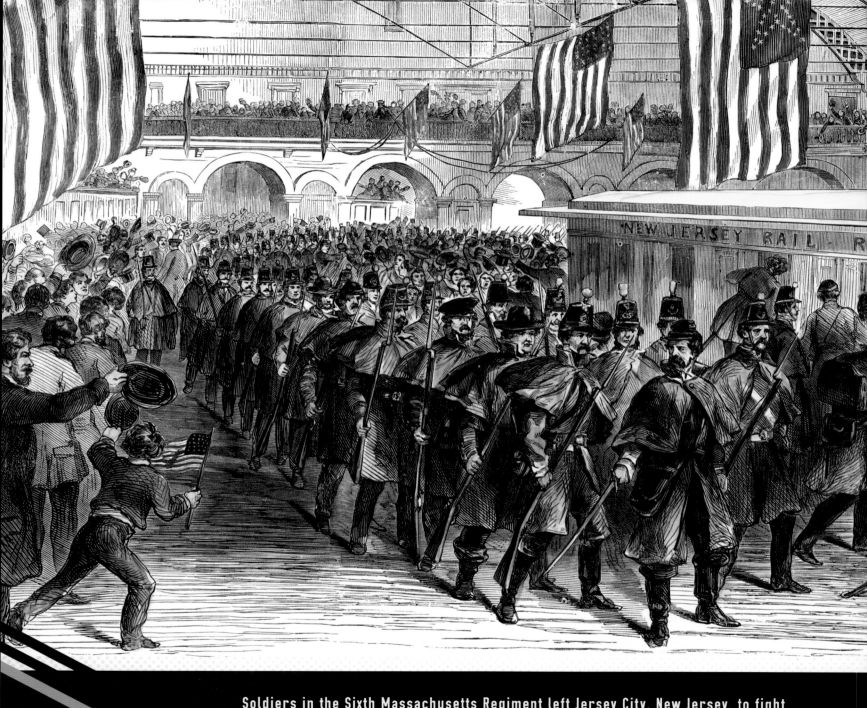

Soldiers in the Sixth Massachusetts Regiment left Jersey City, New Jersey, to fight in the Civil War in 1861.

"THE WAR IS OPEN"

The day after Fort Sumter fell, President Lincoln issued a proclamation officially declaring the attack to be an armed act of rebellion against the United States. At the same time, he issued an order for states to begin forming militia units. The US Army at the time consisted of approximately 16,000 men, many of whom were in the West fighting or chasing Native Americans. Lincoln asked for 75,000 troops to assemble in Washington, DC, as soon as possible for the purpose of suppressing the rebellion. Congress met on July 4 and issued its own proclamation of war, calling for a half million volunteers and authorizing pay for three months' duty.[1] The action spurred Confederate president Davis to call for 100,000 Southern men to rally to the cause.[2] Quickly, four more

Southern states joined the Confederacy—Virginia, North Carolina, Tennessee, and Arkansas.

Many Americans seemed to accept the coming of war with a sense of relief, followed by a frenzy of rejoicing. People in cities and towns, North and South, rushed into the streets waving flags and singing patriotic songs. Farm boys, shop clerks, and mechanics rushed to join rapidly forming military units. War offered a chance to escape the dull routine of life and to replace it with "thrilling scenes . . . sublime daring, heroic achievement and grim horrors," as described in an article in *Scientific American*.[3]

Even those who had no intention of rushing into battle saw the coming of war as a positive good, something the nation needed. "Thank God the war is open," South Carolina governor Francis Pickens said.[4] Virginia governor Henry A. Wise told people of the South, "You want war, fire, blood to purify you; and the Lord of Hosts has demanded that you should walk through fire and blood."[5] The Northern

A HERO'S WELCOME IN NEW YORK CITY

When Major Robert Anderson and his men returned to New York City, they were welcomed as heroes by cheering mobs. New Yorkers had gone flag-crazy in anticipation. The city was ablaze with them, and Broadway was described as being almost hidden in a sea of red, white, and blue. A rally in Union Square drew approximately 200,000 people, clamoring for a look at the Fort Sumter defenders and their battle flags.[6] One fluttered from a treetop and another lay in the arms of George Washington's statue, astride his horse in the center of the square. New Yorkers had never seen anything like it.

THE STARS AND BARS

People in the South celebrated and waved flags, too—mostly their state flags. The Confederacy and its Stars and Bars, adopted in March 1861, were still too new to be as revered and cherished as the Union and the Stars and Stripes were in the North.

The Confederacy's original Stars and Bars flag had three broad bars, which were red and white, on a field of blue. Seven stars appeared on the flag, representing the first seven states that seceded. Eventually, the Confederate flag depicted two crossed blue bars on a field of red with thirteen stars.

magazine *Harper's Weekly* agreed: "Peace . . . corrupts society; war strengthens and purifies."[7] Cleansing and purifying, mental and spiritual, seemed to be on everyone's minds. It may have had something to do with the religious revival that had swept the nation in the late 1850s. Perhaps the bloodshed of war would wash away the sins of the nation. Many Americans saw the war in exactly those terms. Lincoln had used such religious terms during his campaign. Poet Walt Whitman even referred to Lincoln as the "Redeemer President."[8]

Ultimately, the reasons people chose to fight in the Civil War are many and complex. Historians still debate exactly what combination of political and social circumstances finally pushed the nation into the abyss. One thing is clear, however. Slavery—not states' rights or tariffs or commercial interests—was the primary cause of the war.

In the end, the South claimed the North and the Republican Party, with its obsession over slavery, drove them to secession and war. Vicious attacks by abolitionists, they said, threatened to stir up revolt among the slaves. The overbearing, tyrannical federal government permitted and even encouraged the attacks. Honor played a large role as well. As one Southern spokesperson said, the North intended "to destroy our property and . . . to degrade us and our families to an equality of slaves."[9] Finally, the South based their act of pulling away from the Union on the same concepts Jefferson expressed in the Declaration of Independence as the basis of the American Revolution of 1776—"It is the Right of the People to alter or to abolish [their government], and to institute new Government, laying its foundation on such principles and organizing its powers in such form, as to them shall seem most likely to effect their Safety and Happiness."[10]

In an address on July 4, 1861, Abraham Lincoln spoke for the Union, not just a Northern collection of states. "On the side of the Union, [the war] is a struggle for maintaining in the world, that form, and substance of government, whose leading object is, to elevate the condition of men—to lift artificial weights from all shoulders . . . and to afford all, an unfettered start, and a fair chance, in the race of life."[11] He was speaking of slavery. The Confederacy, he went on, was an "illegal organization." Southern secession was not a noble quest for freedom, as the revolution of 1776 had been, but a crime against the Union and its people.

President Lincoln with General George B. McClellan on the battlefield at Antietam in Maryland

Although many were happy war had finally erupted, by its end, the Civil War claimed the lives of hundreds of thousands of soldiers.

He could not allow a few "discontented individuals" to destroy the Union he had vowed to preserve and protect.[12]

The causes behind the American Civil War had been brewing for a number of years prior to 1861. Slavery was at the heart of the matter. As the nation expanded and developed, life, liberty, and the pursuit of happiness were rights that were not extended to every individual living in the United States. As the nation stepped into the Civil War, the two sides would spend more than four years battling over the issues that had caused them to come to the brink of war.

TIMELINE

1619
Dutch traders bring the first African-American slaves to Jamestown.

June 11, 1776
The First Continental Congress appoints a committee to draft the Declaration of Independence.

July 13, 1787
Congress passes the Northwest Ordinance, which structures settlement of the Northwest Territory.

September 17, 1787
The Constitution is signed, guaranteeing legal protection for slave owners.

May 22, 1856
Representative Preston Brooks attacks and canes Senator Charles Sumner.

1857-1858
Republican candidate Abraham Lincoln runs for Senate in Illinois.

March 6, 1857
The US Supreme Court rules on the *Dred Scott* case.

February 6, 1858
A debate over slavery results in the most infamous brawl in the history of the US House of Representatives.

July 1803

The Louisiana Purchase from France doubles the area of the United States.

March 6, 1820

President James Monroe signs the Missouri Compromise.

September 1850

The Compromise of 1850 admits California into the Union as a Free State.

January 4, 1854

The Kansas-Nebraska Act is introduced to the Senate, which creates the territories of Kansas and Nebraska.

October 16, 1859

John Brown leads a failed attempt to overtake a US Army arsenal at Harpers Ferry, Virginia.

November 6, 1860

Abraham Lincoln is elected to the presidency.

December 20, 1860

South Carolina secedes from the United States.

April 12, 1861

The Civil War begins with the Battle of Fort Sumter.

ESSENTIAL FACTS

KEY PLAYERS

- Abraham Lincoln was elected president in 1860, sending the South into secession and open hostility against the Union.

- Jefferson Davis, formerly both a US representative and senator from Mississippi and also secretary of war under President Franklin Pierce, was elected first president of the Confederate States of America in 1861.

- William Lloyd Garrison, a leading abolitionist, pushed for the emancipation of slaves through his speeches and newspaper, the *Liberator*.

- John C. Calhoun, a senator from South Carolina, was instrumental in encouraging Southern secession and organizing the Nashville Convention of Slave States in 1850.

KEY CAUSES OF THE CIVIL WAR

SLAVERY
At the heart of the Civil War was the battle over slavery. The South was dependent upon slave labor to maintain its plantation economy. Many Northerners believed slavery was wrong and that it should be abolished.

EXPANSION OF THE NATION
As the United States acquired large portions of land, the question arose whether these new territories would eventually become slave states or Free States. This led to bitter disputes and rioting in territories such as Kansas.

ABOLITIONIST MOVEMENT

The growing abolitionist movement in the North helped raise awareness of the mistreatment of slaves. Abolitionists condemned slavery on moral grounds and sought the immediate emancipation of slaves.

IMPORTANT TECHNOLOGIES

- The cotton gin revolutionized the speed and profitability of processing cotton, making cotton the South's largest crop. Slavery became economically indispensable.

- Railroads and the invention of high-speed printing presses and the telegraph sped up the spread of information. These gave birth to dozens of daily newspapers, which shaped public opinion during the last decade before the Civil War.

- Photography was in its infancy in the years just before the Civil War, yet it quickly became a powerful propaganda tool.

QUOTE

"In your hands, my dissatisfied fellow-countrymen, and not in mine, is the momentous issue of civil war."

—*Abraham Lincoln during his first inaugural address in 1861*

GLOSSARY

ABOLITIONIST
A person who wants to end slavery.

COMPROMISE
A settlement of differences by a partial yielding on both sides.

EMANCIPATION
The act of freeing an individual or group from slavery.

FANATIC
A person who is carried away beyond reason by his or her feelings or beliefs, usually toward a controversial matter.

FUGITIVE
A person who runs away to avoid recapture.

GARRISON
A military camp, fort, or base.

INSURRECTION
A hostile rebellion.

MANIFEST DESTINY
The belief in the 1800s in the inevitable territorial expansion of the United States.

MARTYR

A person who gives his or her life for a noble or religious cause.

MILITIA

A military force made up of nonprofessional fighters.

ORDINANCE

A law or statute.

PROPAGANDA

Information that carries facts or details slanted to favor a single point of view or political bias.

PROVISO

A clause in a contract or document by which a condition is introduced.

RATIFY

To formally approve or adopt an idea or document.

SECESSION

The formal withdrawal of one group or region from a political union.

TARIFF

A scheduled set of prices, fees, duties, or taxes on imported or exported goods.

ADDITIONAL RESOURCES

SELECTED BIBLIOGRAPHY

Fleming, Thomas. *A Disease in the Public Mind: A New Understanding of Why We Fought the Civil War*. New York: Da Capo, 2013. Print.

Freehling, William W. *The Road to Disunion: Secessionists Triumphant*. New York: Oxford UP, 2007. Print.

Goldfield, David. *American Aflame: How the Civil War Created a Nation*. New York: Bloomsbury, 2011. Print.

Stampp, Kenneth M. *The Causes of the Civil War*. New York: Simon, 1991. Print.

Ward, Geoffrey C. (with Ric and Ken Burns). *The Civil War: An Illustrated History*. New York: Knopf, 1990. Print.

Wineapple, Brenda. *Ecstatic Nation: Confidence, Crisis, and Compromise, 1848–1877*. New York: HarperCollins, 2013. Print.

FURTHER READINGS

Dodge Cummings, Judy. *Civil War*. Minneapolis: Abdo, 2014. Print.

Miner, Craig. *Seeding the Civil War: Kansas in the National News, 1854–1858*. Lawrence, KS: UP of Kansas, 2008. Print.

Sandler, Martin W. *Lincoln through the Lens: How Photography Revealed and Shaped an Extraordinary Life*. New York: Walker, 2008. Print.

WEBSITES

To learn more about Essential Library of the Civil War, visit **booklinks.abdopublishing.com**. These links are routinely monitored and updated to provide the most current information available.

PLACES TO VISIT

Fort Sumter National Monument
Visitor Education Center
340 Concord Street
Charleston, SC 29401
843-577-0242
http://www.nps.gov/fosu/index.htm
Visitors to Fort Sumter can walk the fort's walls, examine some of the original artillery pieces, explore the museum, and enjoy the same views the fort's defenders saw.

Harpers Ferry National Park
Visitor Center
171 Shoreline Drive
Harpers Ferry, WV 25425
304-535-6029
http://www.nps.gov/hafe/planyourvisit/directions.htm
The park offers a variety of John Brown and Civil War–related sites and activities.

SOURCE NOTES

CHAPTER 1. SHOWDOWN AT FORT SUMTER: THE BRINK OF WAR

1. Nelson D. Lankford. *Cry Havoc! The Crooked Road to the Civil War, 1861.* New York: Viking, 2007. Print. 75.

2. James McPherson. "A Brief Overview of the American Civil War—A Defining Time in Our Nation's History." The Civil War Trust. Web. 1 Oct. 2015.

3. Guy Gugliotta. "New Estimate Raises Civil War Death Toll." *New York Times.* New York Times. 2 Apr. 2012 Web. 10 Oct. 2015.

CHAPTER 2. SLAVERY IN A "MORE PERFECT UNION"

1. Richard A. Sauers, et.al. *Civil War Chronicle: 150th Anniversary.* Lincolnwood, IL: Legacy Publishing, 2011. Print. 12–13.

2. Eric Foner. *The New American History.* Philadelphia, PA: Temple University, 1997. Print. 14.

3. Ari Helo. *Thomas Jefferson's Ethics and the Politics of Human Progress: The Morality of a Slaveholder.* New York: Cambridge, 2013. Print. 1.

4. Ibid.

5. Ibid.

6. "Slavery." *George Washington's Mount Vernon.* Mount Vernon Ladies' Association, 2015. Web. 5 Oct. 2015.

7. "The Declaration of Independence," *The Charters of Freedom.* National Archives, n.d. Web. 5 Oct. 2015.

8. Thomas Fleming. *A Disease in the Public Mind: A New Understanding of Why We Fought the Civil War.* New York: Da Capo, 2013. Print. 52.

9. Edward J. Larsen and Michael P. Winship. *The Constitutional Convention: A Narrative History From the Notes of James Madison.* New York: Random House Modern Library, 2005. Print. 147.

10. "Northwest Ordinance, July 13, 1787." *Historical Documents Celebrating the 200th Anniversary of Ohio Statehood.* National Archives, 2015. Web. 5 Oct. 2015.

11. Richard Beeman. *Plain, Honest Men: The Making of the American Constitution.* New York: Random House, 2009. Print. 329–30.

12. John R. Vile. *The Men Who Made the Constitution: Lives of the Delegates to the Constitutional Convention.* Lanham, MD: Scarecrow Press, 2013. Print. 305.

13. Catherine Drinker Bowen. *Miracle at Philadelphia: The Story of the Constitutional Convention, May to September 1787.* New York: Little, Brown and Company, 1986. Print. 201.

CHAPTER 3. EXPANDING NATION, EXPANDING PROBLEMS

1. "Louisiana Purchase, 1803." *Office of the Historian.* US Department of State, 2015. Web. 5 Oct. 2015.

2. Richard J. Behn. "The Founders' Faith." *Lehrman Institute.* Lehrman Institute, 2015. Web. 5 Oct. 2015.

3. "Manifest Destiny." *History Channel.* History Channel, 2015. Web. 5 Oct. 2015.

4. "James Monroe: Life in Brief." Miller Center of Public Affairs, University of Virginia, 2015. Web. 5 Oct. 2015.

5. Ibid.

6. "Nat Turner's Rebellion, 1831," *Africans in America*. PBS, 2015. Web. 5 Oct. 2015.

7. Thomas Fleming. *A Disease in the Public Mind: A New Understanding of Why We Fought the Civil War*. New York: Da Capo, 2013. Print. 93.

8. Ibid. 93.

9. Richard Griswold del Castillo. "War's End: Treaty of Guadalupe Hidalgo." *U.S.–Mexican War*. PBS, 2015. Web. 5 Oct. 015.

CHAPTER 4. THE CALIFORNIA QUESTION AND ANOTHER COMPROMISE

1. David Goldfield. *America Aflame: How the Civil War Created a Nation*. New York: Bloomsbury, 2011. Print.

2. Thomas Fleming. *A Disease in the Public Mind: A New Understanding of Why We Fought the Civil War*. New York: Da Capo, 2013. Print. 172.

3. Ibid. 182–83.

4. "Fugitive Slave Act." *History Channel*. History Channel, 2015. Web. 5 Oct. 2015.

5. "The Emancipation Proclamation." *Civil War Trust*. Civil War Trust, 2014. Web. 15 Sept. 2015.

6. John Buescher. "Keep Your Top Eye Open." *Teaching History*. National History Education Clearinghouse, 2015. Web. 15 Sept. 2015.

7. Tom Colarco. *Places of the Underground Railroad: A Geographical Guide*. Santa Barbara, CA: ABC–CLIO, LLC, 2011. Print. 37.

CHAPTER 5. NEW MEDIA AND PUBLIC OPINION

1. "American Newspapers, 1800–1860: An Introduction." *University Library*. University of Illinois at Urbana–Champaign, 2015. Web. 15 Sept. 2015.

2. Ibid.

3. Lorman A. Ratner and Dwight L. Teeter, Jr. *Fanatics and Fire–Eaters: Newspapers and the Coming of the Civil War*. Urbana, IL: University of Illinois, 2003. Print. 9.

4. Ta-Nehisi Coates. "What This Cruel War Was Over." *The Atlantic*. 22 June 2015.

5. "The Southern Argument for Slavery." *Ushistory.org*. The Independence Hall Association in Philadelphia, 2014. Web. 15 Sept. 2015.

6. "Anti-Slavery Movement in the United States." *National Library of Australia*. National Library of Australia, 2015. Web. 15 Sept. 2015.

7. Thomas Fleming. *A Disease in the Public Mind: A New Understanding of Why We Fought the Civil War*. New York: Da Capo, 2013. Print. 103.

SOURCE NOTES
CONTINUED

8. Elizabeth D. Huttman. *Urban Housing Segregation of Minorities in Western Europe and the United States.* Durham, NC: Duke University, 1991. Print. 243.

9. Thomas Fleming. *A Disease in the Public Mind: A New Understanding of Why We Fought the Civil War.* New York: Da Capo, 2013. Print. 100.

10. Dennis E. Frye. "Purged Away with Blood." *Civil War Trust.* Civil War Trust, 2015. Web. 5 Oct. 2015.

CHAPTER 6. BLEEDING KANSAS: THE WIDENING GULF

1. *Precedents Relating to the Privileges of the Senate of the United States.* US Senate. Washington, DC: US Government Printing Office, 1893. Print. 98.

2. "Border Ruffians." *Ushistory.org.* The Independence Hall Association in Philadelphia, 2014. Web. 15 Sept. 2015.

3. "Bleeding Kansas." *History Channel.* History Channel, 2015. Web. 5 Oct. 2015.

4. Thomas Fleming. *A Disease in the Public Mind: A New Understanding of Why We Fought the Civil War.* New York: Da Capo, 2013. Print. 214–15, 217.

5. "Dred Scott's Fight for Freedom." *Africans in America.* PBS, 2015. Web. 15 Sept. 2015.

6. David Goldfield. *America Aflame: How the Civil War Created a Nation.* New York: Bloomsbury, 2011. Print. 139–40.

7. Ibid.

8. "Declaration of Sentiments." *Encyclopedia Britannica.* Encyclopedia Britannica, 2015. Web. 20 Sept. 2015.

9. Brenda Wineapple. *Ecstatic Nation: Confidence, Crisis, and Compromise, 1848–1877.* New York: HarperCollins, 2013. Print. 41–42.

10. David Goldfield. *America Aflame: How the Civil War Created a Nation.* New York: Bloomsbury, 2011. Print. 144.

11. Henry Martyn Flint. *Life of Stephen A. Douglas, United States Senator from Illinois: With His Most Important Speeches and Reports.* New York: Derby & Jackson, 1860. Print. 169

12. Kenneth M. Stampp. *The Causes of the Civil War.* New York: Simon & Schuster, 1991. Print. 105.

13. "Harriet Beecher Stowe." *History Channel.* History Channel, 2015. Web. 4 Oct. 2015.

CHAPTER 7. THE RISE OF LINCOLN

1. David Goldfield. *America Aflame: How the Civil War Created a Nation.* New York: Bloomsbury, 2011. Print. 147.

2. Ibid. 157.

3. "The Campaign and Election of 1860," Miller Center of Public Affairs, University of Virginia, 2015. Web. 5 Oct. 2015.

4. "Platon." *The Richmond Forum.* 17 Nov. 2012. Web. 20 Oct. 2015.

CHAPTER 8. "NO COMPROMISE!"

1. "Mr. Lincoln and the New Confederacy." *New York Times*. New York Times, 26 Mar. 1861. Web. 20 Oct. 2015.

2. *Evening Star Almanac and Hand Book.* Washington, DC: Evening Star Newspaper Company, Jan. 1898. Vol. 4, No. 1. Print. 363.

3. "Abraham Lincoln, First Inaugural Address, Monday, March 4,1861." *Bartleby.com.* Bartleby.com, n.d. Web. 27 Oct. 2015.

4. Ibid.

5. Ibid.

6. David Goldfield. *America Aflame: How the Civil War Created a Nation.* New York: Bloomsbury, 2011. Print. 199.

7. "Fort Sumter Surrenders." *History Channel.* History Channel, 2015. Web. 30 Oct. 2015.

8. Robert Alonzo Brock. *Southern Historical Society Papers.* Virginia Historical Society, 1894. Volumes 22–24. Print. 113.

CHAPTER 9. "THE WAR IS OPEN"

1. John Whiteclay Chambers II. "Civil War (1861–65)." *The Oxford Companion to American Military History.* 2000. *Encyclopedia.com.* Web. 11 Oct. 2015.

2. "March 6, 1861: Confederate Congress Calls for 100,000 Volunteers." *Civil War Gazette.* Civil War Gazette, 6 Mar. 2008. Web. 31 Oct. 2015.

3. "Our History of the War," *Scientific American* May 11, 1861: 297. Print.

4. Charles P. Roland. *An American Iliad: The Story of the Civil War.* New York: McGraw Hill, 2002. Print. 39.

5. David Goldfield. *America Aflame: How the Civil War Created a Nation.* New York: Bloomsbury, 2011. Print. 206

6. David Detzer. *Allegiance: Fort Sumter, Charleston, and the Beginning of the Civil War.* New York: Harcourt, 2001. Print. 311–313.

7. "War as a Schoolmaster." *Harper's Weekly,* 19 Oct. 1861. Print. 658.

8. Charles P. Roland. *An American Iliad: The Story of the Civil War.* New York: McGraw Hill, 2002. Print. 38.

9. Brenda Wineapple. *Ecstatic Nation: Confidence, Crisis, and Compromise, 1848–187.* New York: HarperCollins, 2013. Print. 167.

10. "The Declaration of Independence," *The Charters of Freedom.* National Archives, n.d. Web. 21 Oct. 2015.

11. Adam Goodheart. *1861: A Civil War Awakening.* New York: Alfred A Knopf, 2011. Print. 362.

12. Ibid. 360.

INDEX

ABOUT THE AUTHOR

Michael Capek is a retired teacher and the author of numerous books for young readers, including *Stonehenge* and *The D-Day Invasion of Normandy*. Michael lives in northern Kentucky, just across the river from Cincinnati, Ohio, near Harriett Beecher Stowe's home and sites she visited while researching *Uncle Tom's Cabin*.